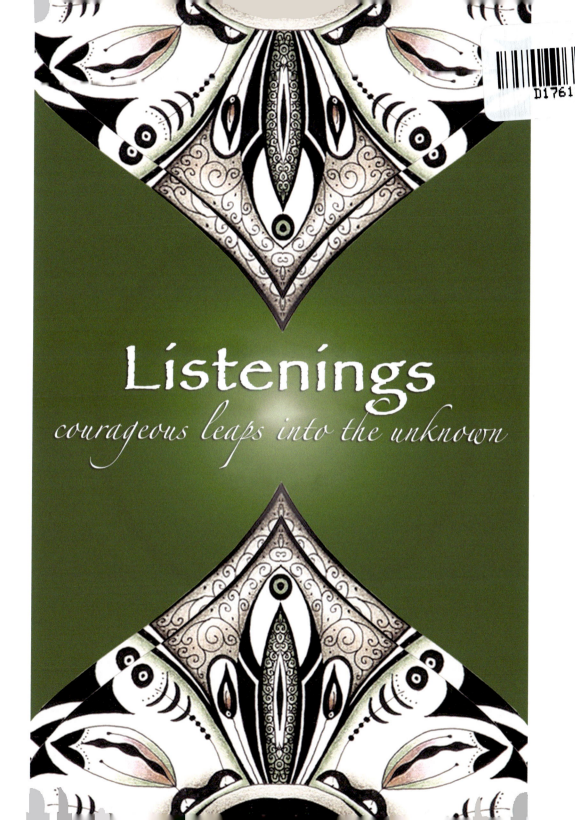

Listenings

courageous leaps into the unknown

To order additional copies of this book, contact:
Xlibris
AU TFN: 1 800 844 927 (Toll Free inside Australia)
AU Local: 02 8310 8187 (+61 2 8310 8187 from outside Australia)
www.xlibris.com.au
Orders@Xlibris.com.au

ISBN: Softcover   979-8-3694-9237-6
        EBook   979-8-3694-9236-9

Print information available on the last page

Rev. date: 24/10/2024

Illustrations and Poetry

by

Melissa Ireland

with gratitude to

A.P. and Nancy, Diana, Jackson, VO, Bee, Amadea,

Mini, Travis, Steph, Rik, Lynn, Liz, Linda, Joan, Marty, Pete,

Francesco, Ronelba, Mushira, Santi and Sanjaya, Godi,

Sydnie, Leonie, Maggie, Molly, Ruby, Serina, Suzi,

Stacy and David

plus… Yuki, Carl, Jane, Jake,

and the art team at Xlibris!

What seems like ages ago, perhaps 40 or more years, I remember someone saying to me, "You are going to write books." This, at the time was one of the most ridiculous things I had ever heard. I barely survived English class in High School, was dyslexic, could read a sentence and look up and not remember a word I had just read, and was focusing my energies on being a visual artist, naming all the images I created, "untitled" to avoid the use of words.

This was not the only place I was avoiding words. I also had no idea how to communicate my feelings so I chose to partner with silence in an attempt to have a friend I felt safe with.

Adding to my successful withdrawal abilities I disappeared to Hawaii. It was there where I met Jackson, who's communication skills made me feel like a pendulum had just traveled to the opposite direction. I had never experienced safe, healthy, criticism coming from unconditional love and drenched in humor. This man was an artist of the verbal dimensions. I was inspired. I had a reference point for communicating that I had never had before. A seed was planted but it would take years of nurturing, watering, and working on the soil conditions before there would be strength and vibrancy in my growth.

My next word teacher appeared in New Mexico. Vivian Gordon is a writer and word artist whose writing embraces the sacred, playfulness, and the visual arts. Her loving presence provided a safe place for me to feel good about challenging myself to name my images as well as to have fun with words. She is a kindred spirit with whom I am grateful to share life.

In 2019 I let go of living in the USA and decided to travel the world volunteering and being creative. I was happily stuck in Australia during covid when I was deeply moved and inspired by the poetry of David Whyte. David's "3 Sundays" zoom events at 3am Australian time were the perfect conditions for what I can say is my first major word blooming adventure The universe added some cosmic humor with his connections to the country of Ireland and the poetry began flowing.

There are other contributors to this evolutionary writing adventure that deserve some credit as well. One of which is the creator of the bucket list…age.

So, with tremendous amounts of insecurity and a gratefulness for a healthy fun-loving dose of courage (as well as some Inner Eco 85% Organic Dark Chocolate), I gift to you my first book, with gratitude for all the visible and invisible human, plant, and animal teachers I have had and their teachers as well and I dedicate this book to a belief in an experience of creativity that is honored, nurtured, loved, and supported, free of the need of suffering. May your creativity bring a smile to the dance of life.

Cheers!
Melissa Ireland

Contents

Poetry

Contents

Art

Courageous Leaps

Out of the vase

Courageous leaps
into the unknown,
the natural order
of spontaneous events,
splash of grace,
life flow

A MOMENTS NOTICE

A moment's notice
A blink of awareness
Infinity knocking
on soul's door

and after that,
a knowing...
that there is no returning
unless accompanied
by a sense of humor!

ONENESS

Oneness,
dressed up as another,
came knocking at my door.
I invited her in for tea.
Together we sat in silence,
sipping possibilities,
watching the steam dance from our cups,
getting to know each other in
dimensions once unknown,
revealing all the other times our paths had crossed,
smiling at the many costumes we had worn,
finally with empty cups,
in a ripened stillness,
we both let out a cosmic giggle
and went our separate ways,
knowing we really had gone nowhere.

GLOWING CONVERSATIONS

BEYOND DEEP

Broken into pieces,
too many to be put back together,
no more moisture left to produce any more tears,
feeling raw beyond time and space,
my pain is
beyond stars and planets,
beyond understanding,
even beyond deep,
and then without being asked to come in,
never voicing where it is from,
as if pleased with being in a place
so pure and open,
silently making itself known,
in it's most subtle essence,
comes joy
blossoming from a seed
known only to the mystery of life.
Existing beyond rhyme and reason,
this blank slate of brilliance
comes carrying a gift,
a gift of the strength to be in two worlds,
as a world of infinite possibilities embraces
a world of pain never to be forgotten,
where only wisdom survives.

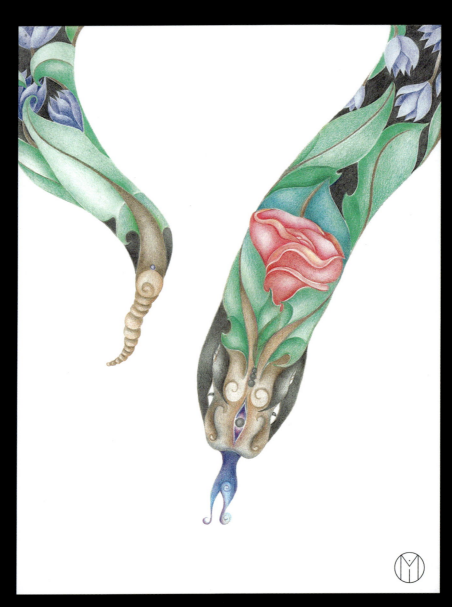

GUARDIAN OF THE GARDEN

OF TRANSFORMATION

MY MEDICINE

My medicine
is a visit from the bush turkey,
a visit from the dragonfly,
the way the tree speaks graciously to me
with her bark and her shadows,
my medicine is the sound of the ocean
when she sings to me
as my body floats with a support
that is pure love,
the sky who calls me outside
to take her photo
as she showcases her colors
behind the clouds, rain, and lightning,
my medicine
is the flower who teaches me
the language of her colors, shapes and
fragrances,
the breeze who visits me
with a whispering touch
and reminds me of the power of being
gentle,
my medicine
is the feel of the black sand
on the beach in la Palma
covering my feet with a warmth
that can heal a fractured foot,
the banyan
who's trunk provides a place for me
to step inside her,
my medicine
is the laughter I experience
when Francesco changes his image
on the phone when we are talking
into funny looking creatures,
the heart shaped cloud
calling my attention
as I sit on top Mount Coot-Tha,
the rattlesnake
who chooses not to bite me
when I blindly come too close to her,
my medicine
is my creativity and my fear
peacefully co-existing,
my vulnerability and my humor
in conversations with wisdom,
and my insecurity
embracing the unknown with courage,
my medicine
is life

PROTECTING THE SEED OF LIFE

CONTENT

Content for years
watching you come and go,
cheering you on in your adventures,
adapting to the alone time,
with an enthusiasm bathed
in curiosity, grace, and artistic flair.
Birthing inner happiness from the seeds of creativity.

The breath of subtleties took center stage,
allowing the familiar to evolve
into an invitation for a new beginning.
Blessed with gentle nurturing,
I embraced the disappearing act
woven by the grace
of an unknown universe.

Can you forgive me?
I did not fall in love with another,
I fell in love with the mystery of life.

11

BELONGING

Standing there,
no longer an expectation
in someone else's performance.

Standing there
in her alone nest,
nestled between the branches
of the tree of life,
the curtain rises
and she gazes into the audience,
and she sees…

those who were sure they knew
what she was going to say and do,
for she had spent lifetimes giving hints
and clues, and she sees…

an empty seat,
untainted from anything
that had gone before,
an empty seat,
not resisting the visitation
of a warm body,
an empty seat,
where she can sit in belonging
and enjoy the show,
as she dances upon the stage.

SHARING BREATH

ALONE

How could I pretend
to be alone
when I share my breath
with every living thing.

PERHAPS

Perhaps....
artists create to dance with reality,
that ever changing effervescence
that welcomes infinity
with a loving embrace.

This dance,
free from self-esteem
and recognition needs,
free from the illusions
of success and failure,
and gratefully free from "make a living",
blesses inward adventures and mysteries
with colors and shapes
that can surprise even the most experienced traveler.
Perhaps artists create
for just a simple moment of intimacy,
a nurturing pause,
where a gentle breeze can take center stage,
announcing peace as the leading lady.
Perhaps artists create
in the infinite presence that they are,
where effort gives way to all that is
with a smile.

DESIRE

I tried to eliminate desire.
Just wanted to see if I could take a break
from it's comings and goings.

Sometimes it would show up so exquisitely dressed
that as an artist I could not resist a sincere exploration.

Other times it was subtle,
gently leading me to a cup of
the perfect tea,
or a walk outside.

Then there was the time where desire
took several years to deliver the goods,
and another time where it took 40 years!
I must have been too busy
earning a masters degree
at the University of Patience
to realize so much time had passed!

And then there have been times where it just floated by
like a cloud, not quite interesting enough to put attention on it,
or maybe it was, and I was just too wrapped up
in some other delicacy of life.

So with my focus on just what is,
I said goodbye to desire.
I ran the other way when I saw it,
or quietly tiptoed around it.
Other times, I played around with the idea
that it was there, but I had no intention
of engaging with it.

The more I tried to look the other way,
desire made itself so subtle,
that the slightest move was drenched in it.
And then one day
I heard the universe say
"Good Luck!!!"

THE MENU

The first time I saw you
was in the dessert section
I pretended I had been to the restaurant many times,
but actually it was way out of my league.
Still, I paid the price.
The sweetness was unrecognizable, confusing,
and yet knowable all at the same time.
The taste lingered for years,
visiting in dreams,
and sometimes surfacing at the most surprising times!
Curiosity accompanied each visit way beyond nine lives.
I still wonder what one of the dishes in the appetizer
section might be like,
or…
on a very courageous day, what planet the main course
would put me on!

LIFE COMES

Life comes,
disguised as an exuberant variety
of transportation services
to take you
from here
to there!

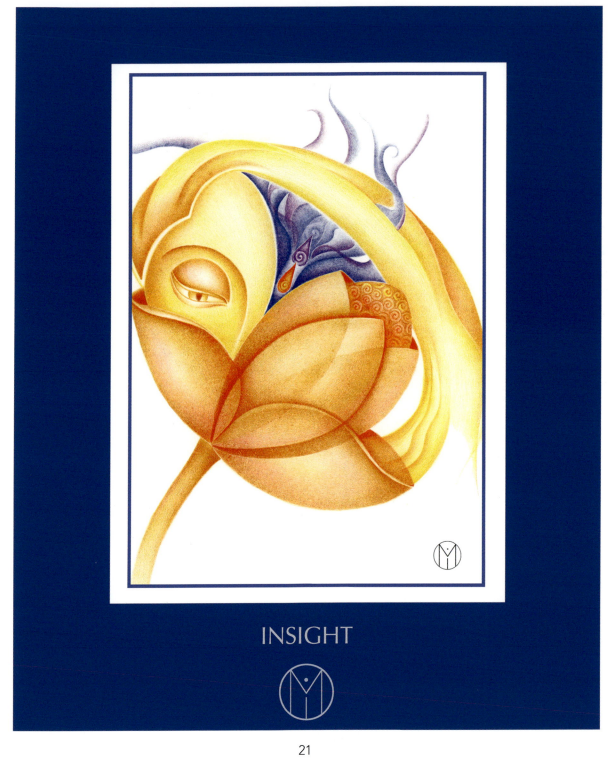

INSIGHT

EASE

My relationship with ease
keeps growing.
At first, we just had glimpses
of each other.
Then there was
one of those
intense moments
where sparkles
rested in the stillness
and the breath of a soft
gentle breeze
that carries words
of wisdom,
invited me
to not be a visitor
but to choose
to be at home in
these soothing colors.

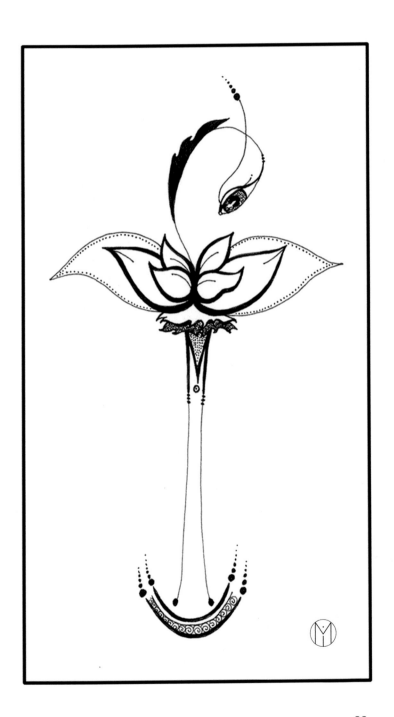

A POWERFUL GIFT

The most powerful gift
I was given,
was the gift to be alone.
Not in separateness from you,
not in loneliness,
and not in fear,
just alone.
Alone to sense
nature's many voices.
Alone to feel a love
that has no boundaries.
Alone to hear wisdom's choice
for what is needed next,
and alone enough to know
that I am not
alone.

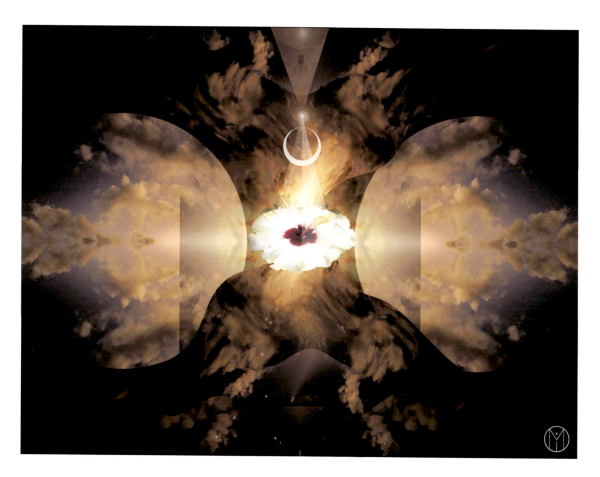

THE FLOW

Living through sensations
wrapped in an eternal now,
flowing from one story to another,
feeling the safety and wisdom of forever....

I breathe flowers and fragrances,
feel barks and breezes,
vibrate with bird songs and whale tunes,
and dance synchronicity

THE NOT TOO DISTANT PRESENT

Now, in the not-too-distant present,
while life transforms
from untitled to one of poetic stories
embracing cosmic humor…

the words that come silently
from my heart,
flow down through my fingertips,
magically energizing my pen,
whose ink flows forth onto this piece of paper,
generously donated by the very being
who I am partnering with
to keep us both alive,
for this brief and sacred moment,

each flowing word,
vibrating with a curiosity,
as we best describe the exuberance
of embracing a dance with infinity
with a smile that welcomes uncertainty

IT'S A WILD
WORLD

It's a wild world
where we fool ourselves
into thinking
we tamed it!

Dance of the three moons

AIR HEAD

I am leaving my head in the clouds,
allowing it to scatter amongst
the sky and the stars.
Each particle breathes me,
teaching me to walk lightly
on this earth,
feeling the subtleties of each moment,
allowing sensations to dance
a nurturing dance,
even when sadness is intense.

The air is where I am from,
where I am going,
and where I have never left
and I carry it wherever I go,
to remind me,
that I am friends with infinity,
with you,
and with all that is.

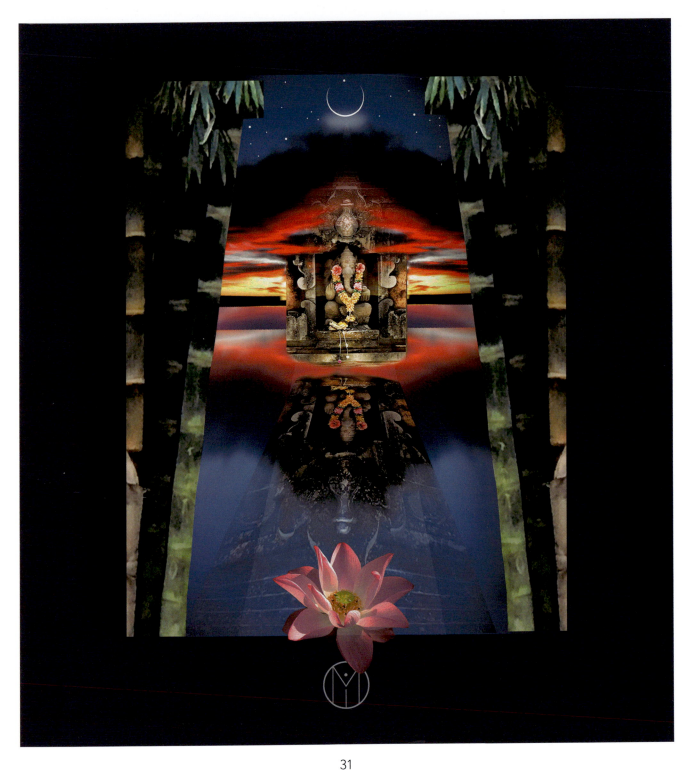

APOLOGIES

I apologize for disappearing,
it is where I go to collect the pieces
that I let scatter the universe
so that I may put them together again
in a work of art that has never existed before.

One that has no voice of the past,
not one iota to distract or tear away
at new beginnings,
nor one that contains any hints of the future,
for those will show themselves
through sparkling serendipities
and a gentle unfolding
while I dance with the mysteries
who constantly teach me
new dance steps.

33

APPEARANCES

Her appearance in this life slipped past
the conscious intention makers
of the world, and instead,
she chose to come into the world
by have to-s, and be taken care of
by the don't really want to-s.

She searched for sincerity, honesty,
and a safe place to be in her innocence,
as she was blown about in a wind of
confusion and misunderstanding
with communication feasting
on misrepresentation.

Peace coming at last,
when the only person to answer to was herself
and in that intimacy a new life emerged
that included every living thing.

PEACE POTION

35

I DON'T KNOW

I don't know what you want,
and what you need
for it is lingering there,
in the secret stories that you have claimed
from the library of existence,
lingering there as invisibilities
in the silence between us.

My guesses might distort their presence,
sending attentions to unrelated dimensions,
opening conversations of unnecessary un-relatedness.

So I sit in the silence of our souls,
where the stillness of turquoise waters
meets a cloudless sky.
Sitting there in an endless silence
made up of my own stories as well…

both of us surrounded
by the expansive wonders
of an infinite number of possibilities,
and the fragrant ripeness
of an invitation for yet another fresh beginning
that can only be opened
in these galaxies of connectedness
with both of our hearts.

THE BOOK OF THE UNIVERSE

When I complete a phase of my life
it becomes a page of poetry in the book of the universe,
positioned there in any one of its infinite chapters,
whispering to those who need it.

These volumes remind me, that on any of my adventures,
I can use this book as my sacred oracle tool.

Closing my eyes, filling my presence with a fun drenched in love,
then opening the book to any page,
I allow my eyes to glance into the stars and embrace whatever I may see
as sacred symbols that are there to guide me with their gentle,
nurturing humor.

The answer, speaks lifetimes into my being and blesses the moment
while gracefully breathing me on to the next amazing adventure,
that I too, may write with my life, another, and another,
poem from the mystery of existence.

A CLEAN SLATE

Gone is fear, she said.
Gone is the hero's journey,
along with its necessity.
All that is taught
does not exist.

A clean slate
blessed by unknowns,
yes, blessed.

Precious blessings,
of flowers breathing fragrances
into wild hearts
and lights
splashing colors of humor
into souls

illuminating paths
free of the myths
of sunrise and sunset

REMEMBERING

I can go nowhere
or be no one,
without the orchestra of the universe
gracefully blooming melodies
into that infinite space that I am.

Seeing the stars
and knowing they are part of
the life in my DNA sends a magical tingling
to my fingers and toes,

and the colors of the rainbow decorate my spine,
the clouds are my adventures,
and the moon and I glow together
in the night, hearing each other's dreams.

Sometimes, raindrops, masquerading as tears,
gather beneath my eyelids to greet the beauty of the day,
and the wind breathes joy through my dancing limbs.

And the artist in each of us, can be heard whispering,
"we were made to be free in this infinite space".

MYSTERY POTION

THE STRANGER

It has been years
And I am still getting to know
the stranger in me.

I like to welcome her
and share a cup of tea,
listening to the adventures she has had.

She likes to remind me,
and I am so grateful she does,
that whatever story I am entrenched in,
she will lovingly meet me in the next one as well,
though I won't recognize her.

One day I asked her,
"Where do you live?"
"Everywhere!" she said.
Ahhh! She blew her cover!

LETTING GO

We die often enough
so that no matter what the form,
the artistry is felt.
The experience steeped in a humility
that was always there,
(even though we pretend it just arrived).

Letting go,
allowing the grace of a remembering,
that the only reality is uncertainty,
be touched with inspiration,
creating a space for us to return
for the next song,
the next dance,
and the next mystery
with a few new moves.

WHEN, WHERE, HOW, WHY

When I die
is a leap into the oneness of the universe,
may it be an enthusiastic one!

Where I die
is the womb of my next existence,
may it be a nourishing one!

How I die
is my gift to all that is,
may it be a conscious one!

Why I die
is to create another work of art,
may it be an infinite one!

WHERE JOY IS FOUND

Aloneness
breathes the grace
of a nurturing universe
into my lungs
and my soul
with the light and the darkness
that knows no duality,
where joy is found.

GRATEFUL

I am grateful for the water around me
and the rain that comes from above
for giving my soul
a place to swim

I am grateful for the air I breathe
for giving my soul
the wings with which to fly

I am grateful for the earth I inhabit
for giving my soul
a place to walk

I am grateful for the sun and light
for giving my soul
warmth and brilliance

I am grateful for the moon
for giving my soul
reflection and mystery

I am grateful for the animals
for giving my soul
friends that are beyond words

I am grateful for you
for giving my soul
someone to dance with

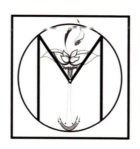

Happily sharing my artwork
and writing....

https://vocal.media/authors/melissaireland

https://instagram.com/melissaireland56

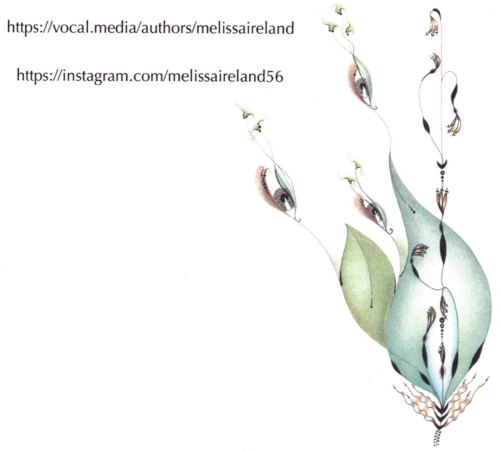